Ocarina Choo-Choo

A beginner's book for the 4 hole alto ocarina

1: Getting Started By Alison Hedger

Teaching five notes: D, E, F#, G and A

This book is for young children in particular, but also for those 'young at heart'! Progress is gentle with lots of tunes to play. The approach is fun, and the recognition of traditional notation should become like a second language.

It is not a good idea to write the note names on the music – ideally children should learn their notes.

At this early stage is profitable to say and clap the short rhythmic patterns of the tunes (using the words given) whilst looking at the written music.

This way, the relation of note values will be gradually assimilated.

The object of OCARINA CHOO-CHOO is for children to make music as soon as possible. However, it is very important that children attempt to produce a good tone from the outset, and learn to play together with regard for others in the group.

The optional CD contains full backing tracks of many tunes to play along with.

© Copyright 2000 Chester Music Limited
Designed by Chloë Alexander • Illustrations by Jan McCafferty • Music setting by Paul Ewers
Printed in Great Britain by Caligraving Limited, Thetford, Norfolk

Chester Music Limited
(A division of Music Sales Limited)
8/9 Frith Street, London W1V 5TZ

Notes used in this book

It is not a good idea for children to be reliant on following fingering diagrams.

It is preferable, even for young children, to recognise which notes to play by their position on the stave.

The drawback with reading diagrams is that the rhythm of the notes is secondary and more often than not ignored.

By looking at traditional notation, both pitch and rhythm are assimilated from the beginning.

Spend a little time discovering the features of the ocarina

Let the children enjoy handling their instruments, looking at the holes, which are all different sizes. Point out the mouthpiece and show how no sound is made if the whistle is covered.

Play a 'bird song' by rapidly covering and uncovering the holes whilst blowing. I call this 'wibbly-wobbly' – it is ideal to try at various points throughout a session. The children love doing it and whilst having fun they are loosening their fingers and discovering the right amount of breath for optimum sound.

Try over-blowing and not much sound is produced!

The notes used in this book, showing their position on the stave in relation to each other

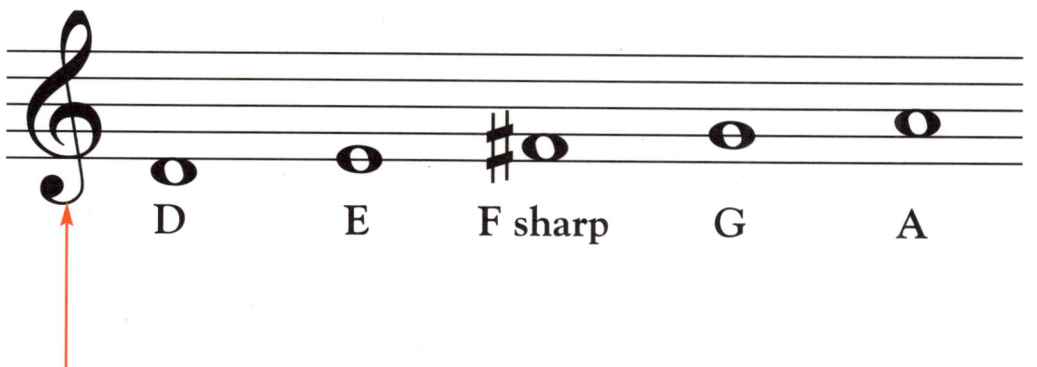

D   E   F sharp   G   A

A curly treble clef sign begins each new piece of music

The stave (five music lines) is divided into equal sections by bar lines:

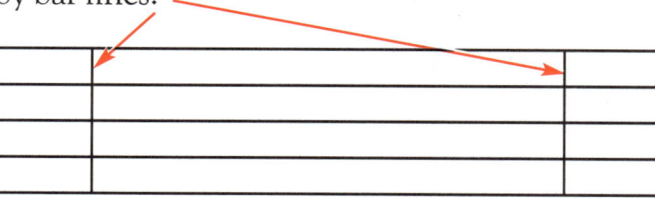

No note is played during a rest, which is silent. Only single beat rests 𝄽 have been used in Book 1.

✓ breath mark

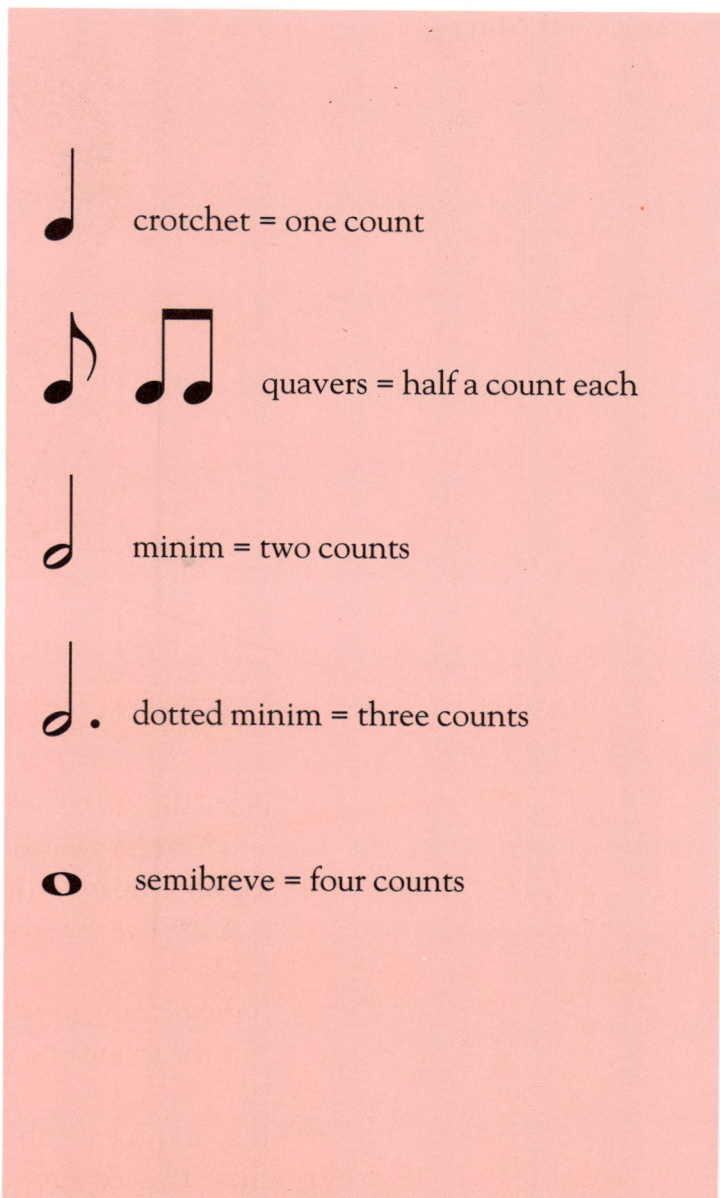

♩ crotchet = one count

♪ ♫ quavers = half a count each

𝅗𝅥 minim = two counts

𝅗𝅥. dotted minim = three counts

𝅝 semibreve = four counts

Correct playing position

Are you holding your ocarina like this?

Holding the ocarina

Place the string over your head. Pick up the ocarina and turn it towards you, so that the four holes are on top and the mouthpiece (whistle end) is close to your mouth. Tilt the string end up.

If the ocarina is near your nose it is too high. Tilt the string end down.

If it sits on your chin it is too low. It should be between these two extremes.

Place both thumbs behind your ocarina. To cover the holes, place fingers one and two (each hand) on the first and second holes. The third fingers are also on the top, but have no holes to cover. They are used to balance the instrument.

It may be comfortable for young players to have their fourth fingers close to, but below the string end.

First attempts at correct blowing

- Sit up straight and hold the ocarina as shown opposite, covering all the holes.

- Press finger pads hard into the holes so no air can escape. (Look for the impression of holes on the fingers.)

- Place the mouthpiece on the bottom lip.
Do not put the mouthpiece too far into the mouth.

- Gently blow – this is D, the lowest note on the ocarina.

Experiment with the children, showing them that tilting the instrument up and down actually alters the note produced. Have fun with this. Ask the children to play the note D with you, in tune! A worthwhile exercise in listening. Low D is actually one of the hardest notes to play, so early mastering of this, getting true pitch and a steady tone will give an excellent skill base in preparation for new notes. Use a chime bar to give you the correct pitch.

Tongue notes from the outset

- Every time a note is played, say 'du' with your tongue.

- Practise tonguing by 'du-du-du-ing' rhythms from well-known songs (e.g. Baa, Baa, Black Sheep). Use the first note D. This will give the children added practice in developing an acceptable tone.

Remember: strong fingers – gentle breath!

Point out that the ocarina is a musical instrument, and any instrument takes time to play properly.

Be positive and encourage gentle steady breath.

There are lots of tunes to practise new notes.

The Ocarina Choo-Choo

Each truck is an ocarina with a note name on the side

A = Agnes
The Anteater

G = Gloria
The Goat

F♯ = Frankie
The Frog

E = Ezra
The Elephant

D = Doris
The Dog

Can you spot the characters in their trucks?
Look out for them all the way through the book!

1

Dance, dog - gie dance!

2

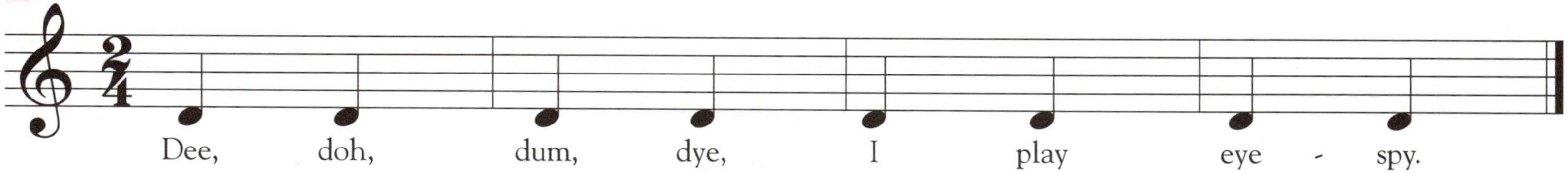

Dee, doh, dum, dye, I play eye - spy.

3

Do - ris the dog got lost in the fog.

4

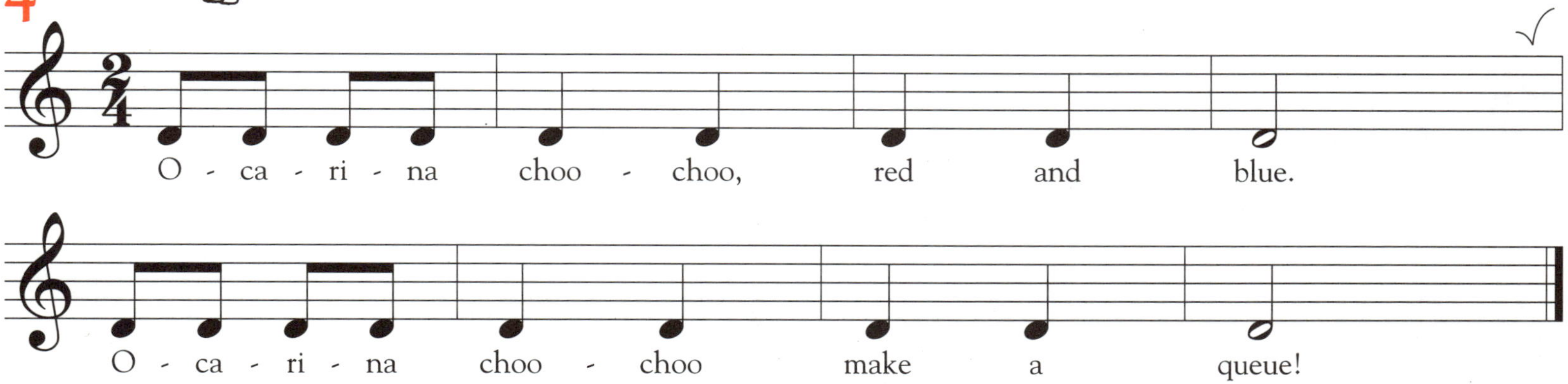

O - ca - ri - na choo - choo, red and blue.

O - ca - ri - na choo - choo make a queue!

5

4 blows on train whistle – made by uncovering all the finger holes.

Will this train go ve - ry fast to - day?

The note D
Below the music lines

Cover all the finger holes

The note E
On the bottom line

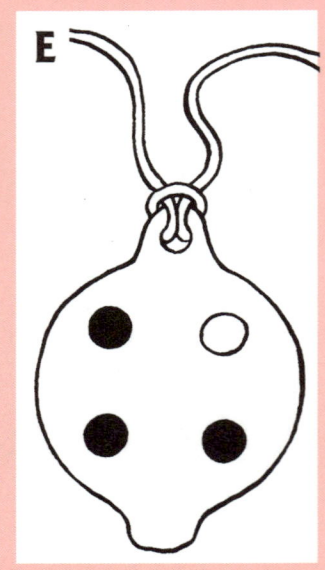

The smallest finger hole is left uncovered (our picture is not to scale)

1 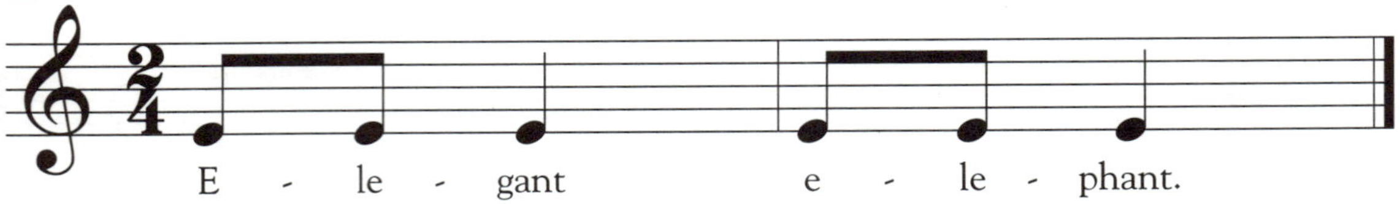
E - le - gant e - le - phant.

2
We all like Ez - ra, 'cause Ez - ra's an e - le - phant.

3
O - ca - ri - na choo - choo, red and blue.

Pas - sen - gers please line up, make a queue!

4
I can keep a stea - dy beat by walk - ing on my four big feet.

1 2 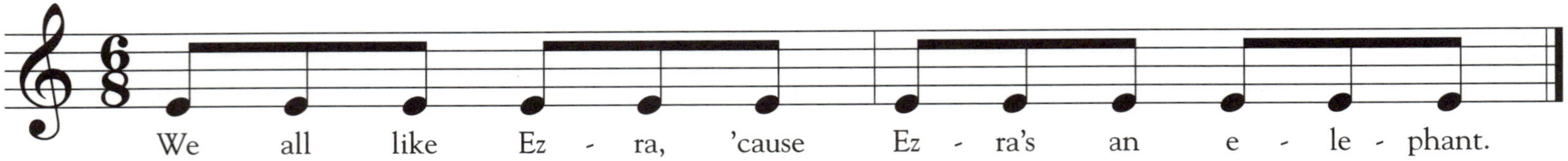 3  4 then a - gain 1 2 3 4 STOP!

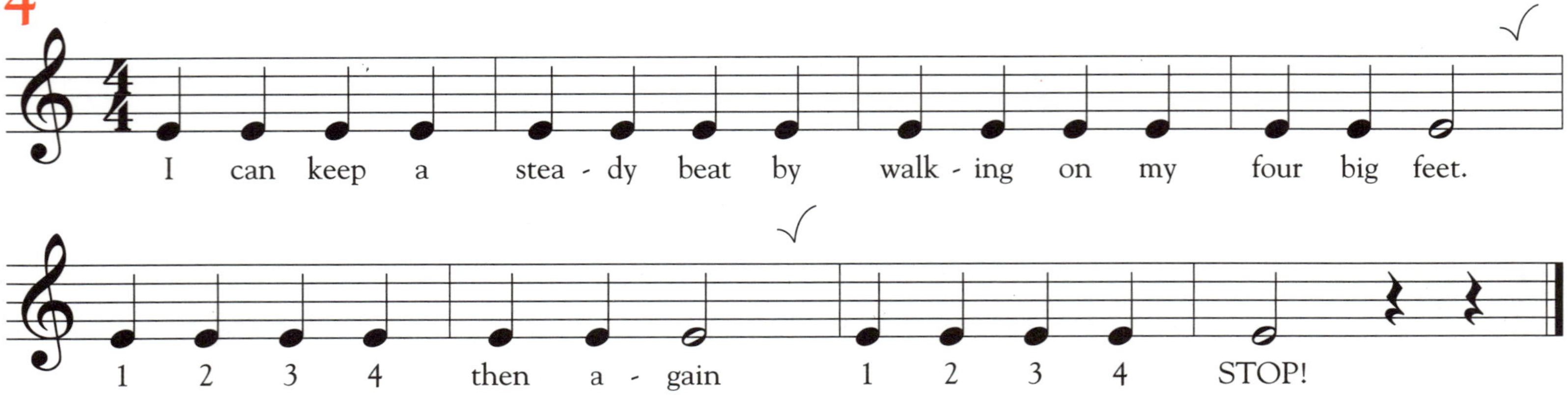

1. E is ea-sy, D's a dod-dle.

2. We are wait-ing at the sta-tion.

3.  Ez-ra wants to dance with Do-ris.

4. Step up, step down.

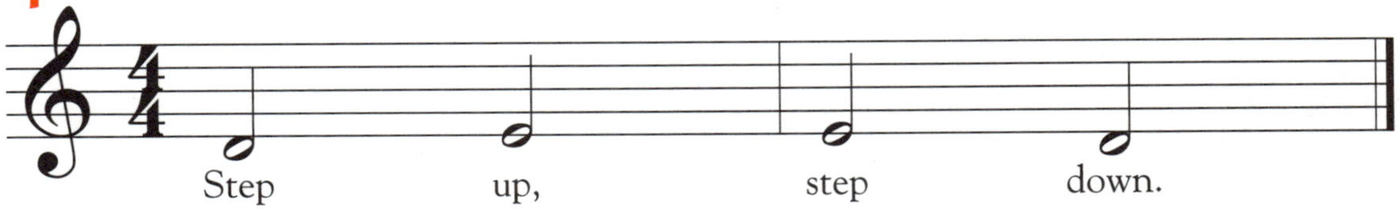

5. I'd like to be at the sea and have big waves crash down on me.

6.  I'm off to Glas-gow to look at the shops.

7. O-ca-ri-na choo-choo, red and blue. Pas-sen-gers please line up make a queue!

Next door neighbours

D E

D
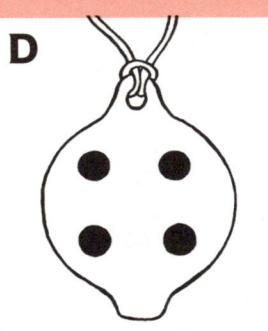

E
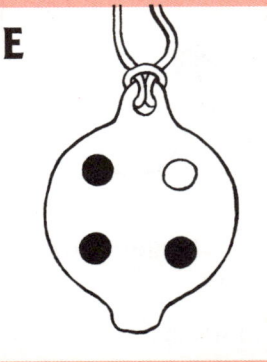

Practise alternating between E and D (thinking: finger up, down; up, down; up, down)

F sharp

Don't forget your third fingers are 'balancers', on top of the ocarina, but they have no holes to cover.

1 Frank-ie the frog is as sharp as can be. He adds up his sums as he catch-es his tea.

2 Frogs are so fun-ny, they hop in the air. They swim and they sit on a log and just stare.

3 F sharp's spe-cial mark is like two rail tracks cross-ing. (shhh)

For fun: practise alternating between E and F♯. Watch your fingers walking!

♯ = the sign for a sharp   𝄽 = a rest worth one count (= ♩) – no ocarina should be heard.

1

2

3

4

Now turn your book upside down to find me!

5

6

7

8

9

Three in a row

Take time to play these three notes

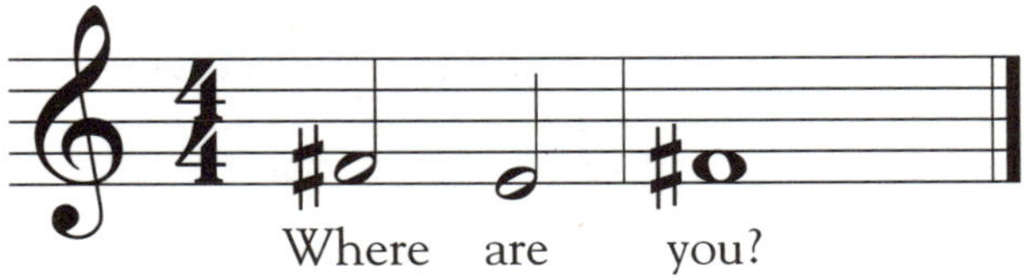

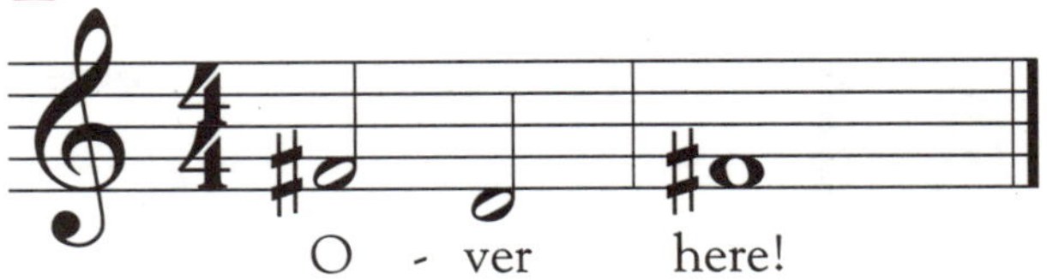

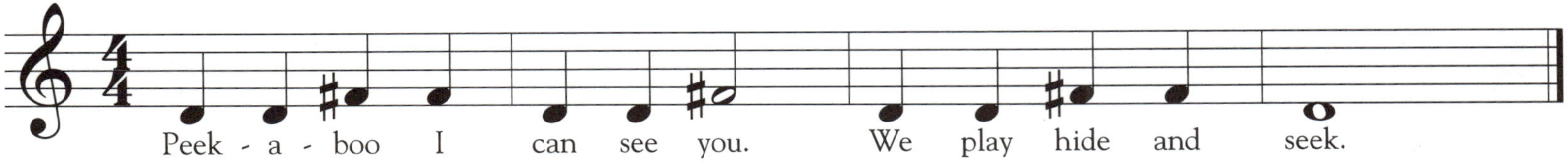

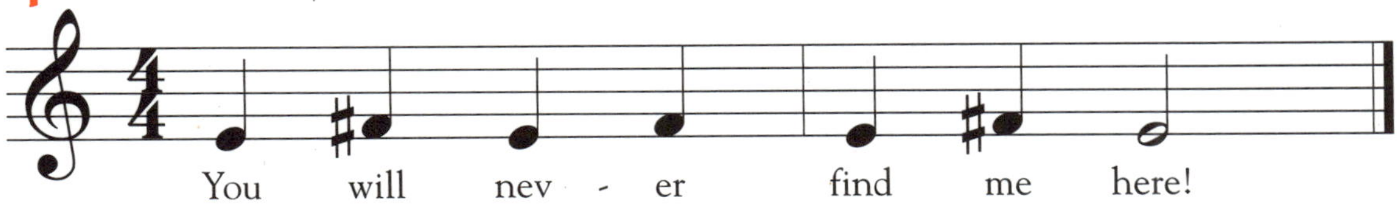

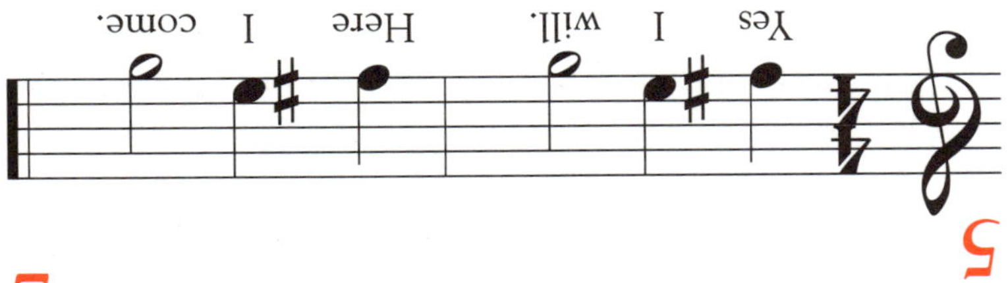

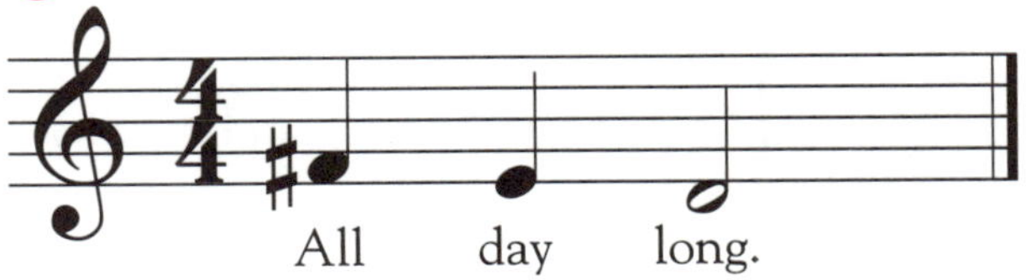

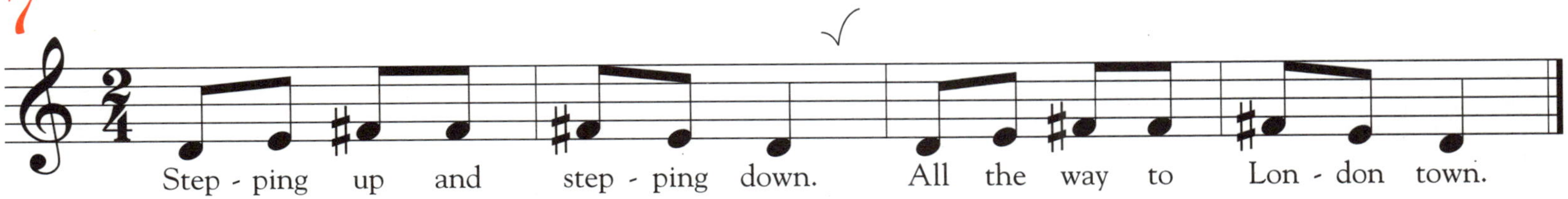

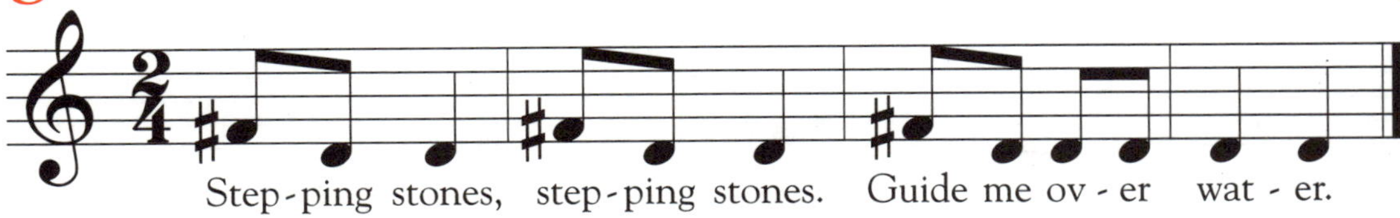

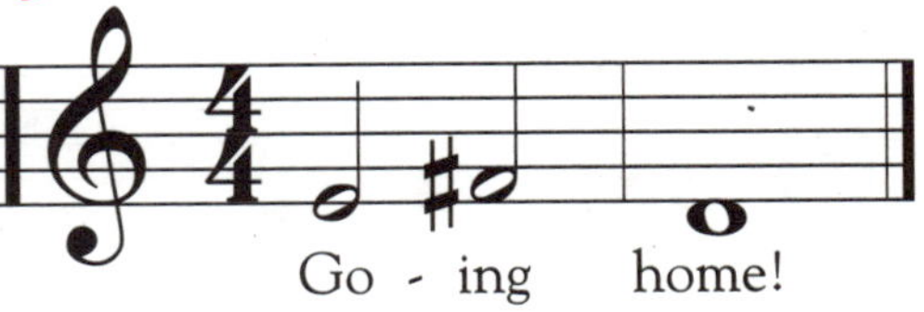

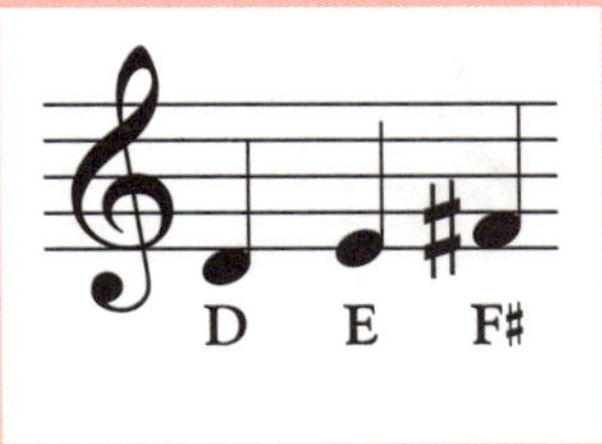

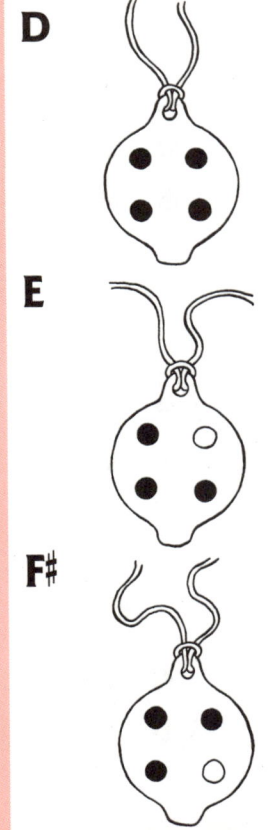

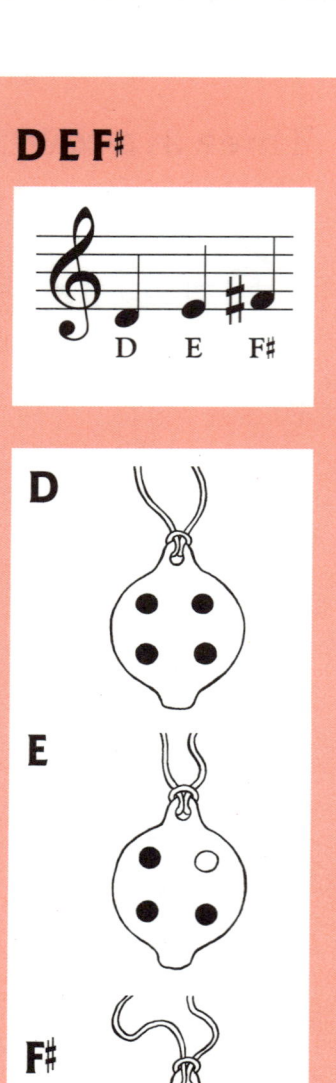

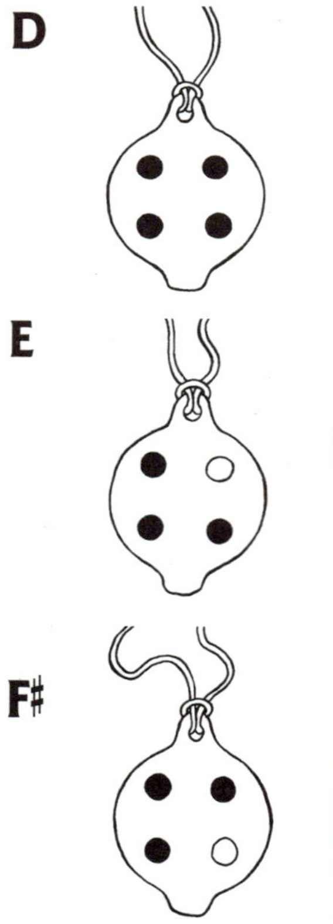

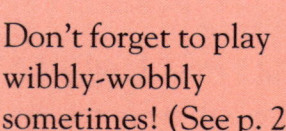

Don't forget to play wibbly-wobbly sometimes! (See p. 2)

1

I play my o-ca-ri-na, I play my o-ca-ri-na.

I play my o-ca-ri-na all day long.

Play in two parts: The last bar can be played as an ostinato (over and over again, whilst the whole tune is being played)

2

1. Ma-bel's go-ing to the fair. Can you choose what she should wear?
2. Dun-ga-rees and her best shirt. Or she could wear her red skirt.

These dots mean play the tune again!

3

Red Rid-ing Hood, walk-ing in the wood

went to see her Grand-ma-ma. Red Rid-ing Hood.

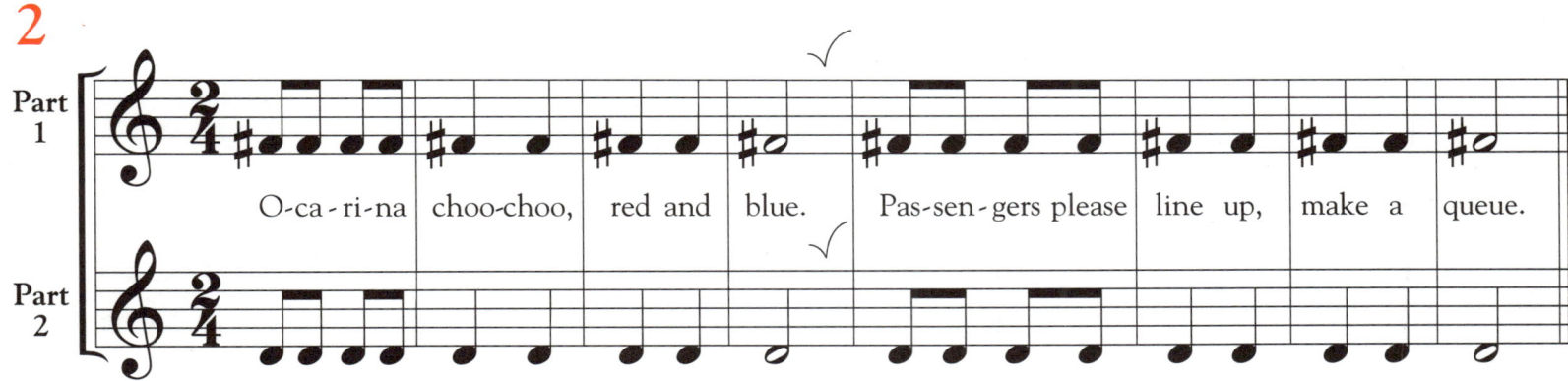

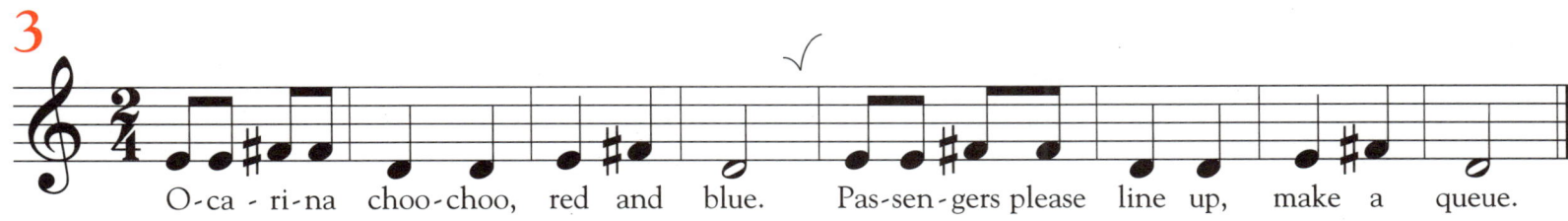

To make a longer piece of music, play song 2, then 3, then 2 again.

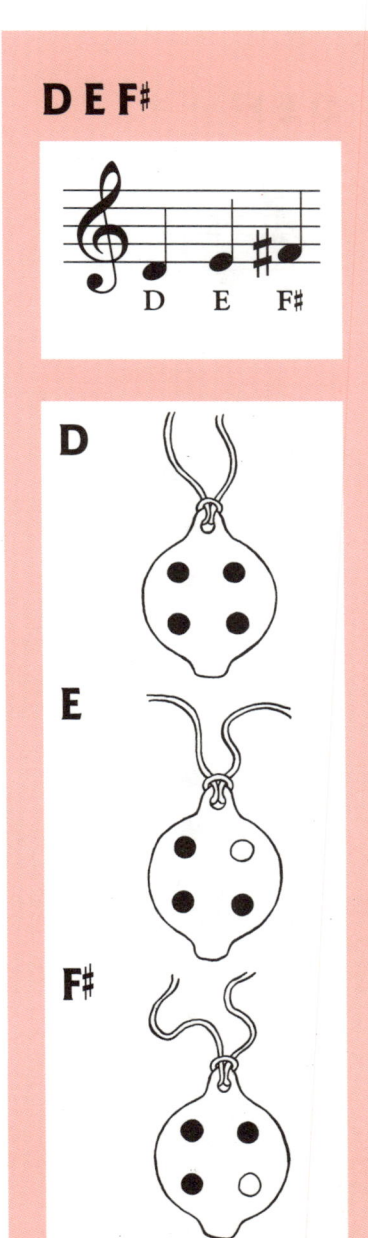

Breathe at the places marked ✓

D E F♯

D

E

F♯

Practise alternating between D and F♯ (think: finger up, down; up, down; up, down)

1

Remember: means play it again

2

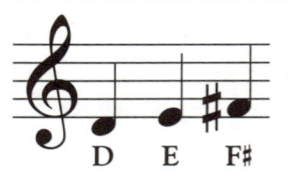

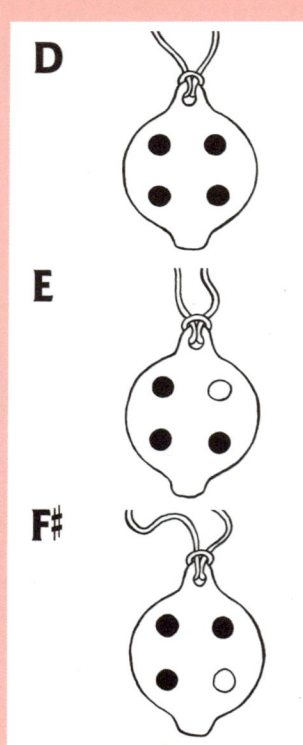

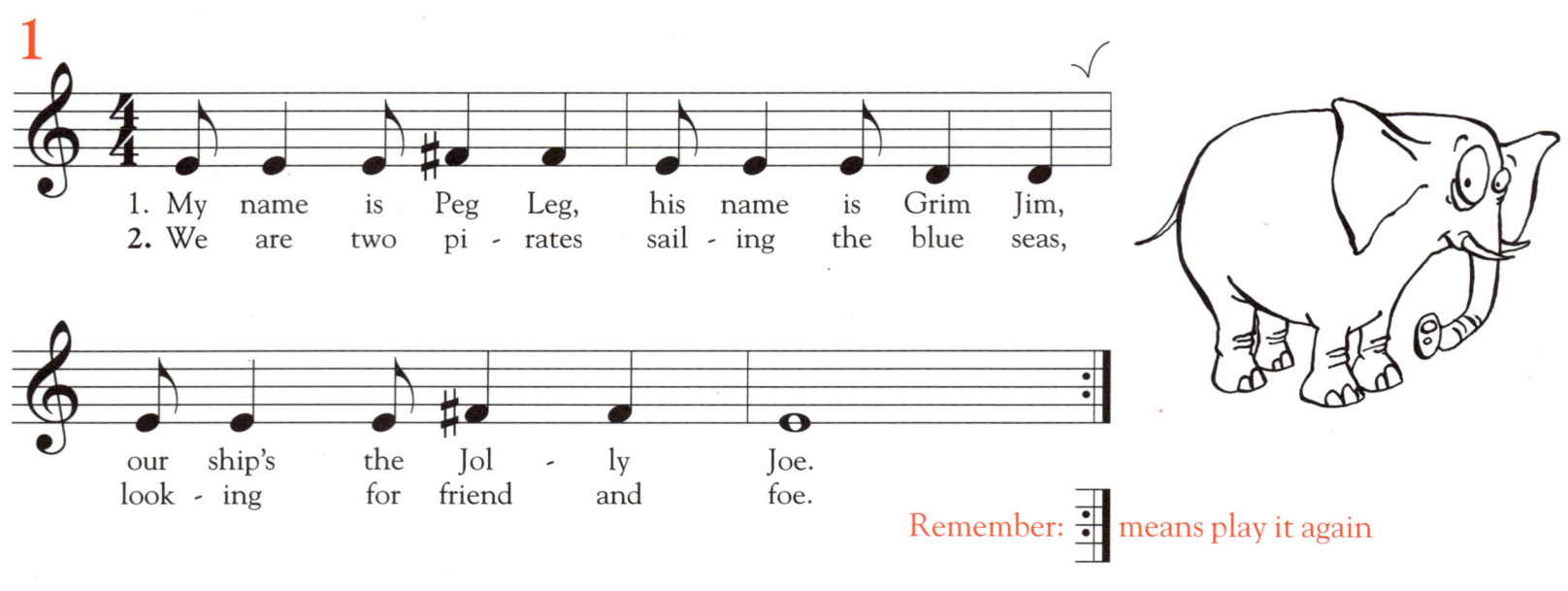

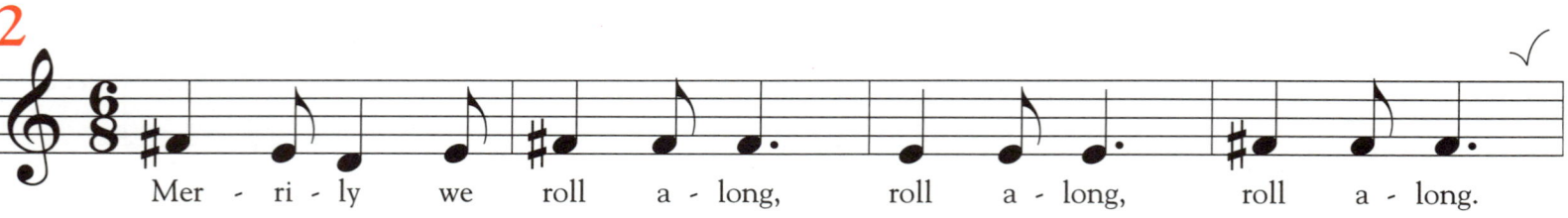

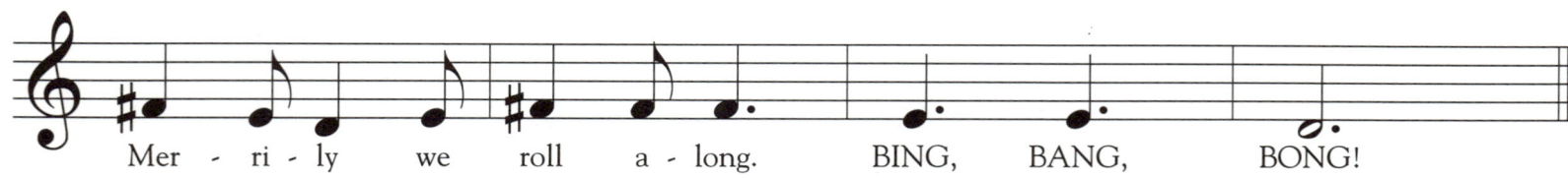

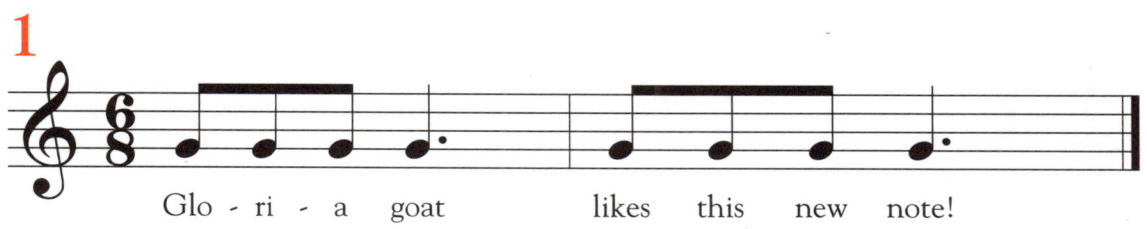
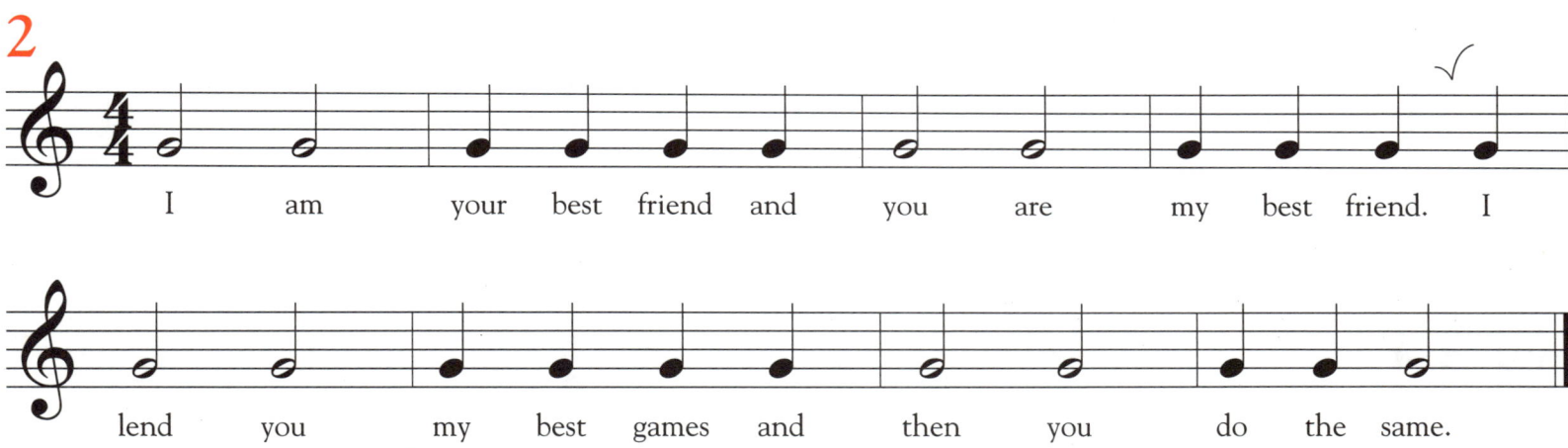

The note G

Don't muddle me up with E (see p. 2)

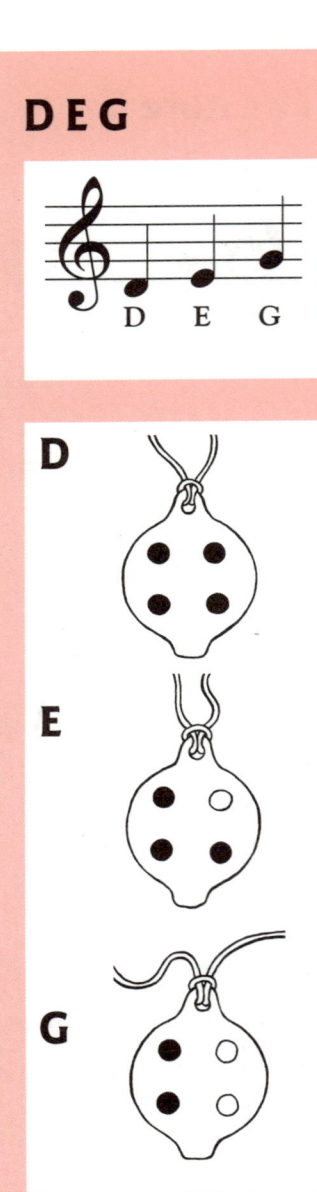

1  Goat jumps up and goat jumps down. Goat runs round and round.

2 Curl-y horns are on my head, but I'd like a hat in-stead!

3 I can hear choo-choo train, as it puffs steam a-gain.

4 Ham-mer, ham-mer in this nail, we must fix the bro-ken rail.
Ham-mer, ham-mer ve-ry hard. Keep the chick-ens in the yard.

1

Slow - ly walk - ing, slow - ly walk - ing, down the hill and up a - gain.

2

I like to tra - vel on this big choo - choo. I like to tra - vel. Would - n't you?

Frankie Frog's sharp sign # can be hung up on the top line, like this:
This will save having to put the sign in front of the F notes

 is still Frankie's own special note: F sharp

3

1. Pease pud - ding hot, pease pud - ding cold. Pease pud - ding in the pot nine days old.
2. Some like it hot, some like it cold. Some like it in the pot nine days old!

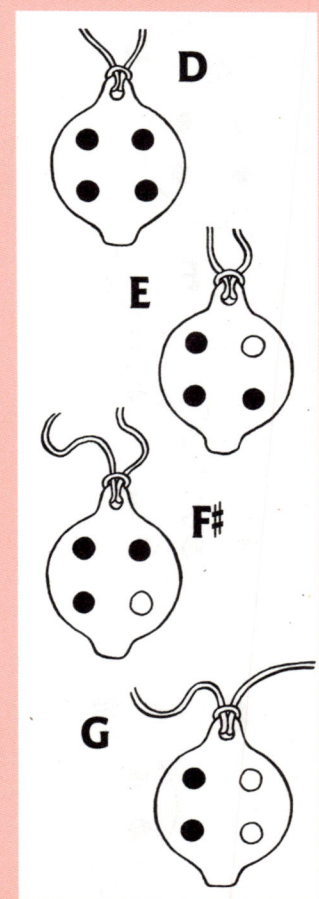

D E F# G

Four notes, all next door to each other

17

D E F# G

For extra practice play these four notes

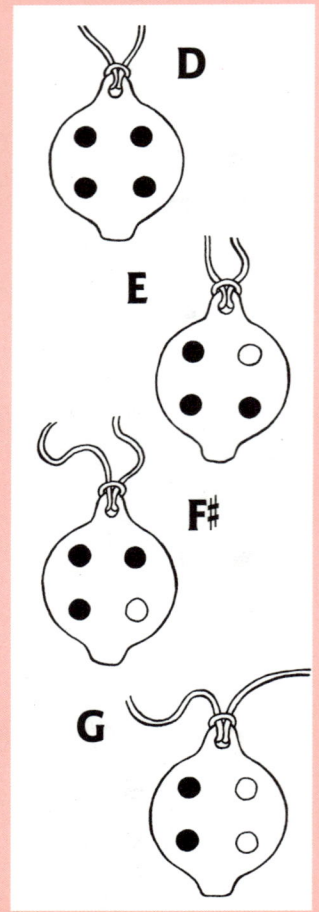

1

Hark, hark, the dogs do bark. Beg-gars are com-ing to town.

Some in jags and some in rags and some in silk-en gowns.

Remember to keep your 'balancers' (third fingers) on top of the ocarina. They have no holes to cover.

2

Knock at the front door Ma-ry, knock at the front door Dee.

Knock at the front door San-cha, Bil-ly must have his tea.

18

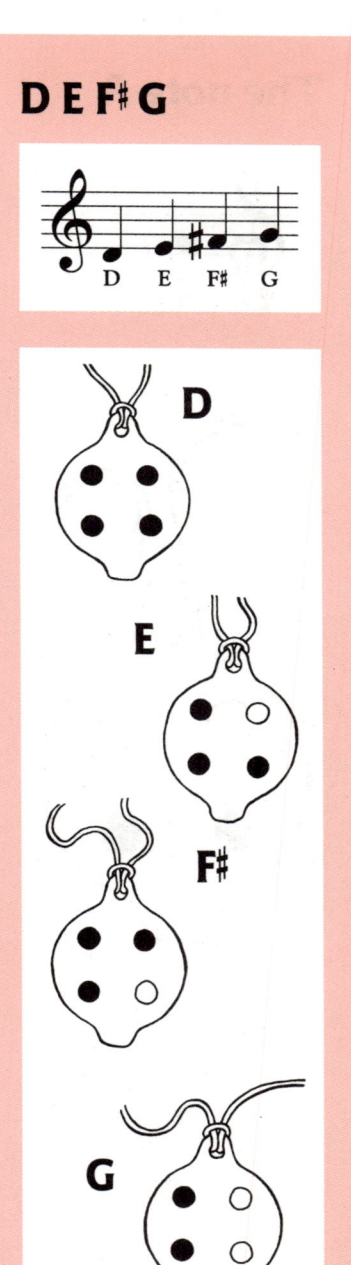

1

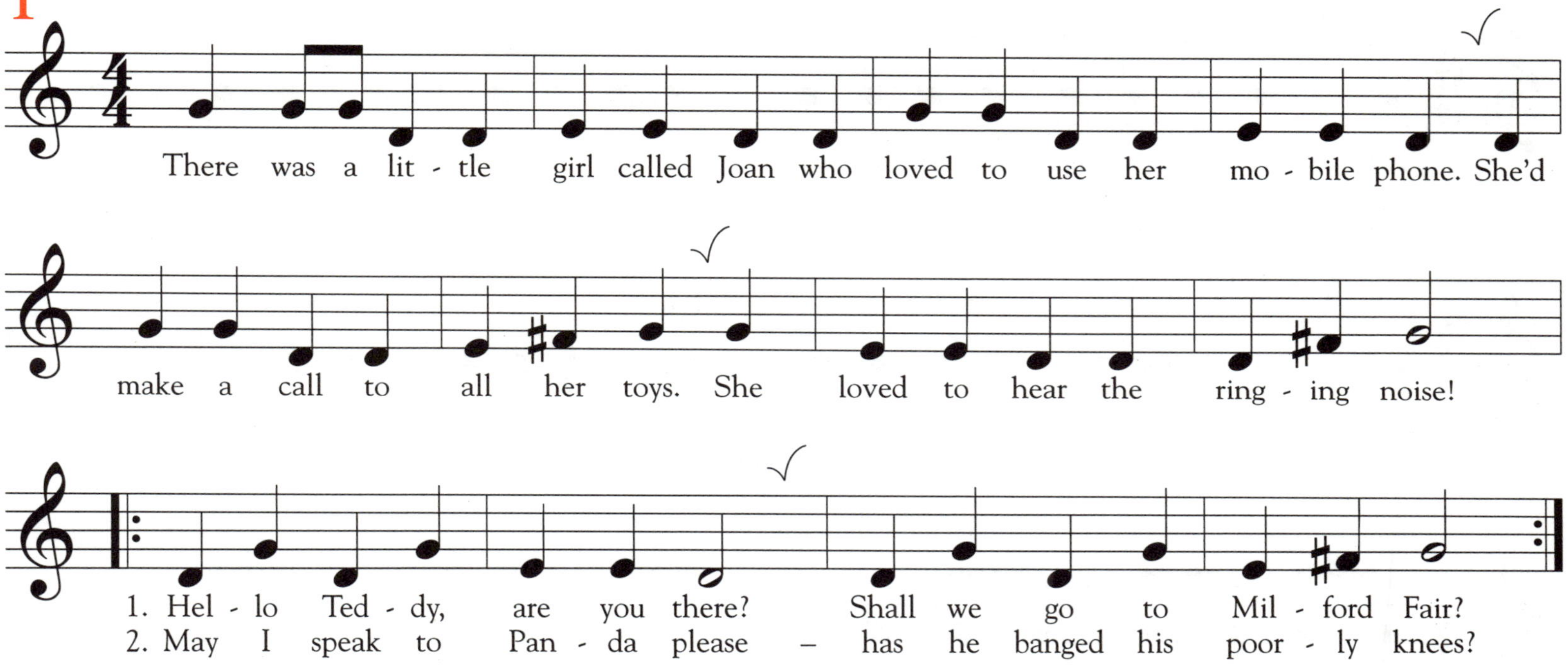

There was a lit - tle girl called Joan who loved to use her mo - bile phone. She'd
make a call to all her toys. She loved to hear the ring - ing noise!
1. Hel - lo Ted - dy, are you there? Shall we go to Mil - ford Fair?
2. May I speak to Pan - da please – has he banged his poor - ly knees?

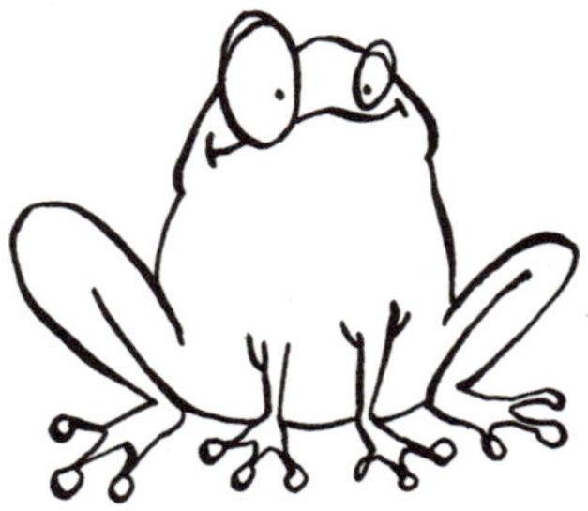

2

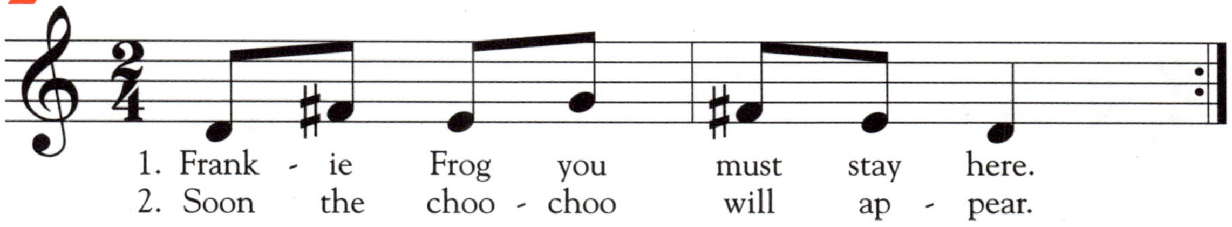

1. Frank - ie Frog you must stay here.
2. Soon the choo - choo will ap - pear.

3

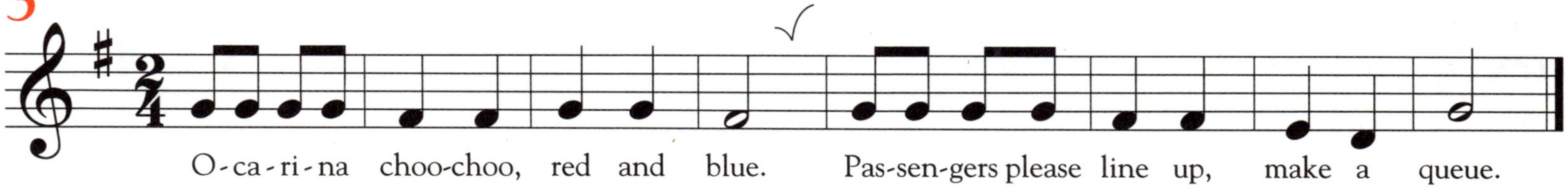

O - ca - ri - na choo-choo, red and blue. Pas-sen-gers please line up, make a queue.

D E F♯ G

D
E
F♯
G

D
E
F♯
G

The note A

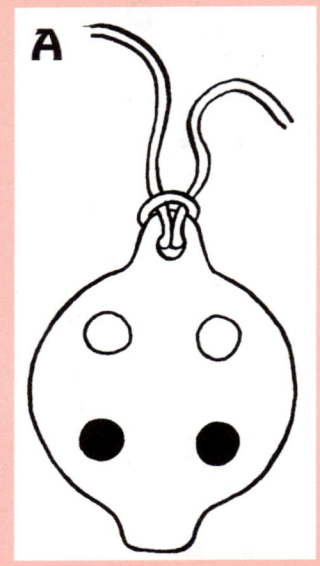

1. Ag-nes the Ant-eat-er snuf-fles a-way. Ag-nes the Ant-eat-er eats ants all day!

2. The choo-choo's whistle
1 2 3 4   1 2 3 4   1 2 3 4   1 and 2 and 3 and 4 and   1 2 3 4

3. Ag-nes wish-es just one thing, that she'd learnt to dance and sing!

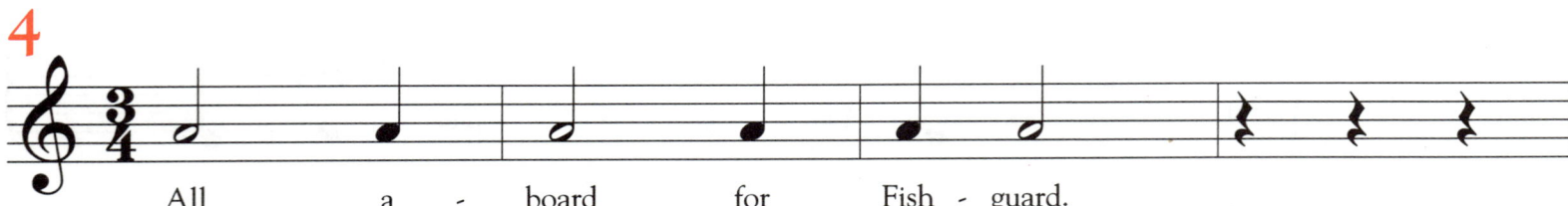

4. All a-board for Fish-guard.

Remember: 𝄽 is a rest – no sound should be heard from the ocarina!

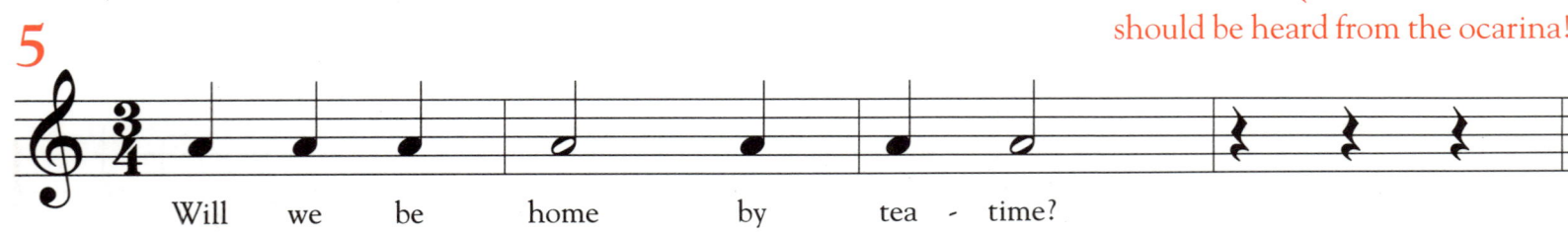

5. Will we be home by tea-time?

1
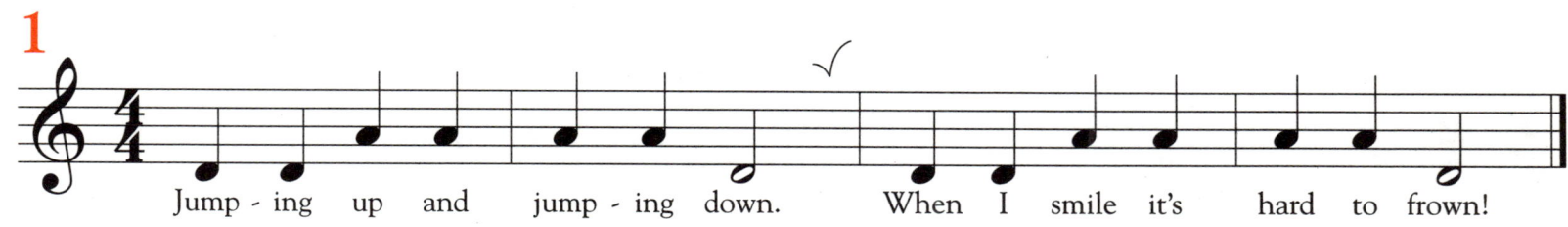
Jump-ing up and jump-ing down. When I smile it's hard to frown!

2
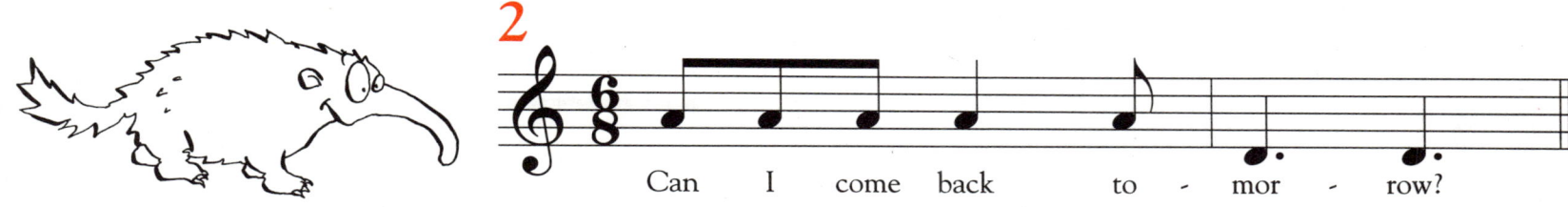
Can I come back to - mor - row?

3
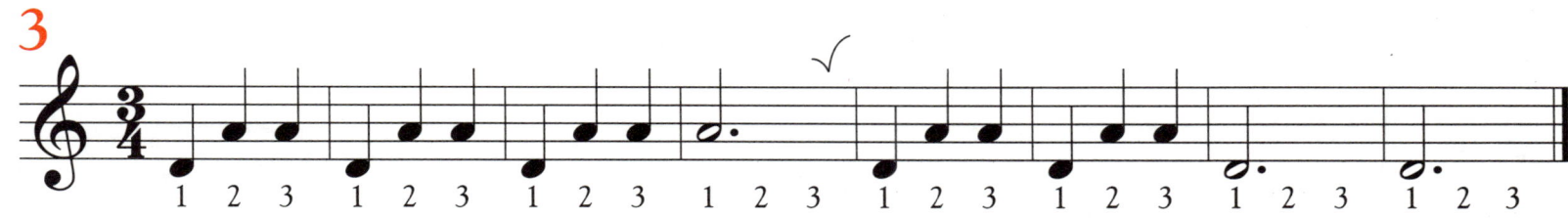
1 2 3 1 2 3 1 2 3 1 2 3 1 2 3 1 2 3 1 2 3 1 2 3

4
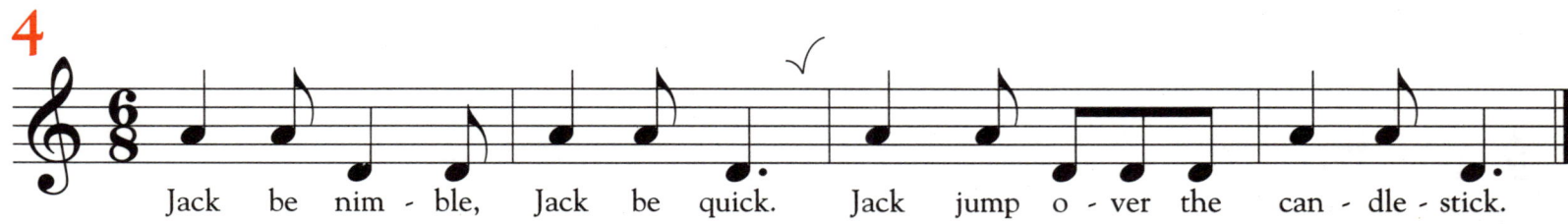
Jack be nim - ble, Jack be quick. Jack jump o - ver the can - dle - stick.

5
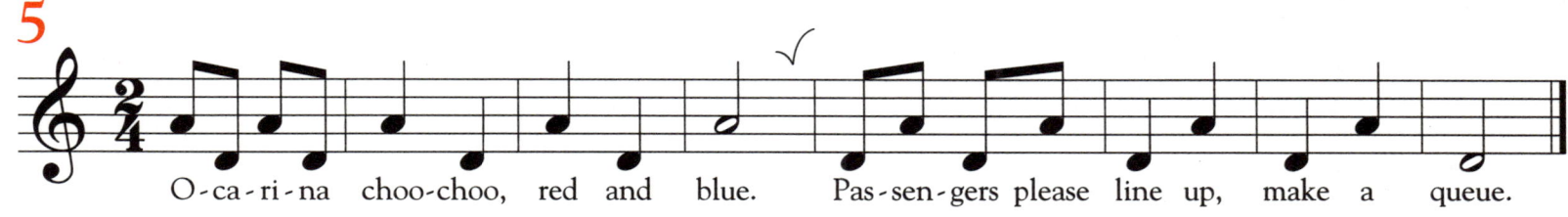
O - ca - ri - na choo-choo, red and blue. Pas - sen - gers please line up, make a queue.

From D to A

What a jump!

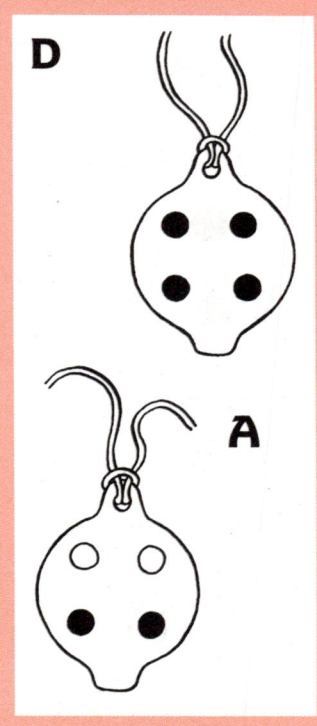

G and A

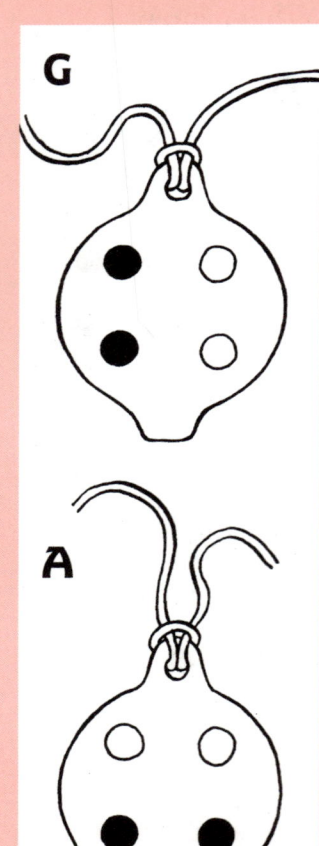

1

Nee - nor, nee - nor.

Alternating between A and G is fun! Watch your fingers go up and down.

2

1. One, two, three, four, five. Once I caught a fish a - live.
2. Six, seven, eight, nine, ten. Then I let him go a - gain.

3

Ag - nes and Glo - ri - a went for a walk. Ag - nes ate ants and the goat chewed a stalk.

4

John - ny get your hair cut, hair cut, hair cut. John - ny get your hair cut, just like me.
Ma - ry cook a pud - ding, pud - ding, pud - ding. Ma - ry cook a pud - ding, just like me.
Gi - gi play the ban - jo, ban - jo, ban - jo. Gi - gi play the ban - jo, just like me.

Can you think of words for more verses?

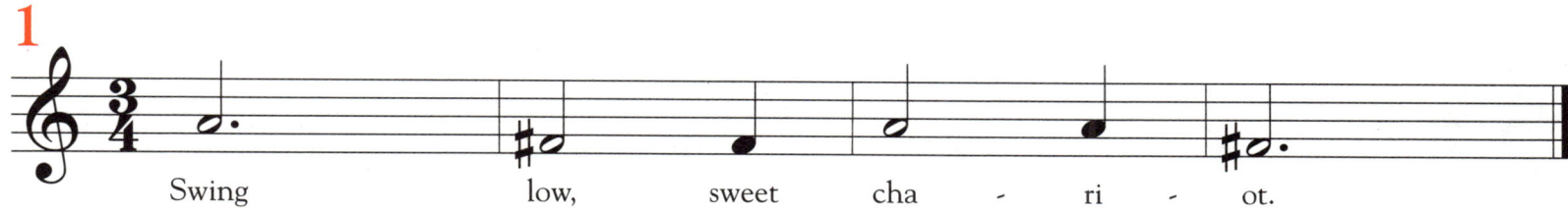

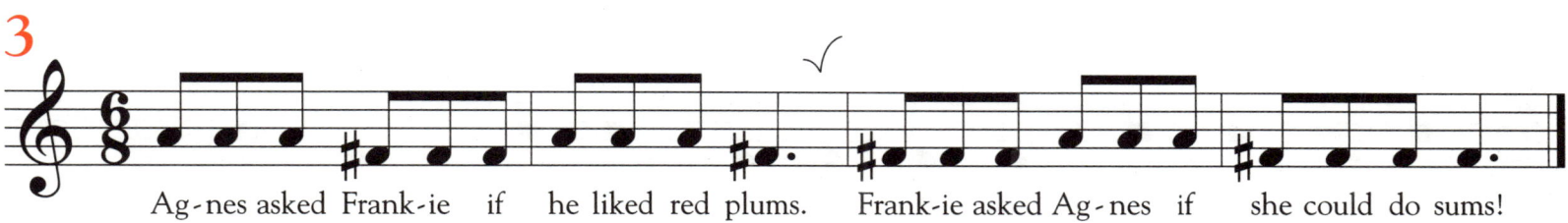
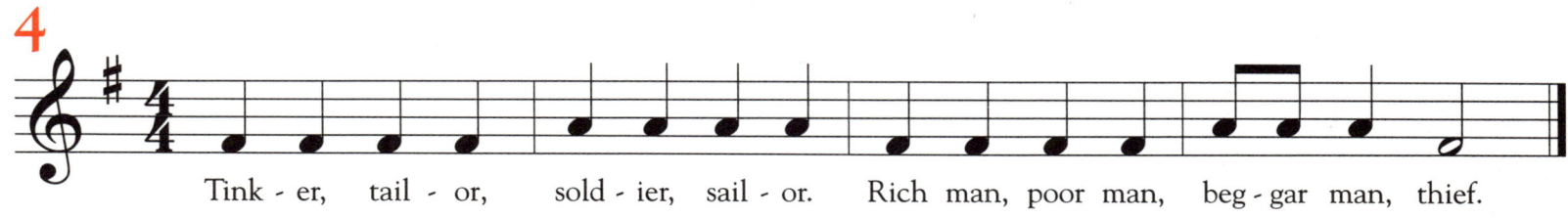

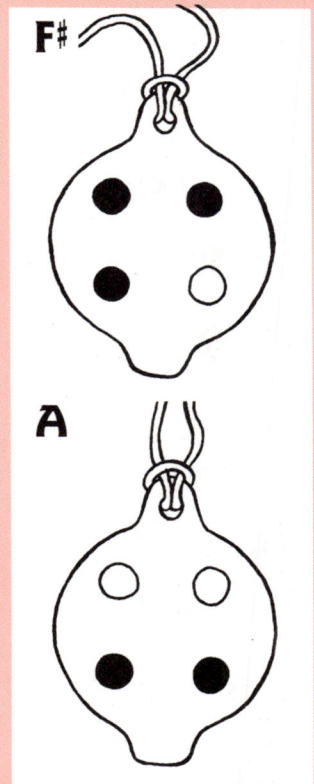

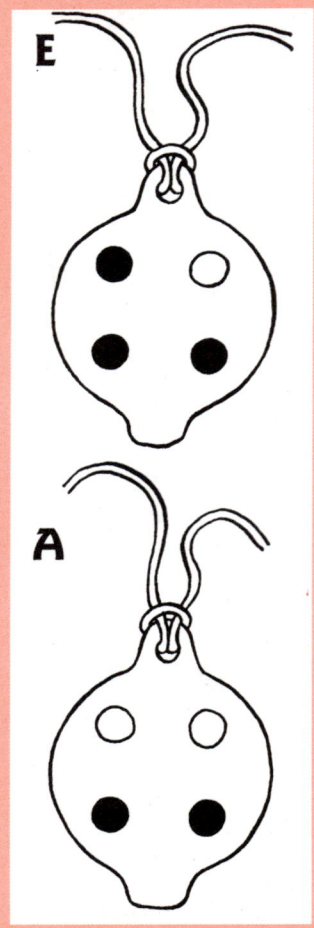

E and A

1

Hel - lo Ez - ra, I'm glad you're here!

2
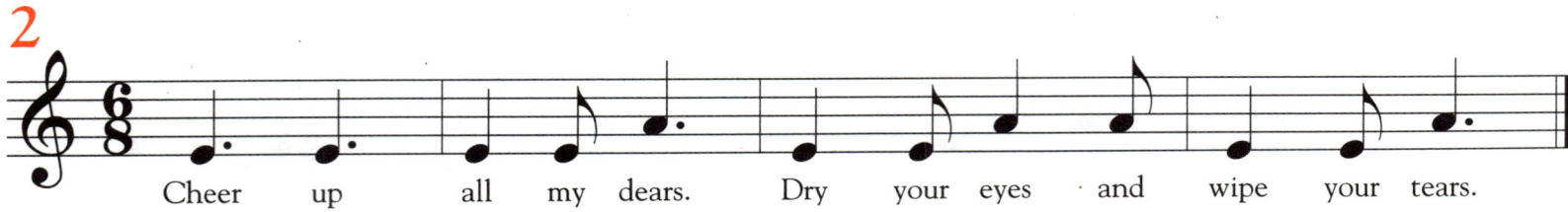
Cheer up all my dears. Dry your eyes and wipe your tears.

3
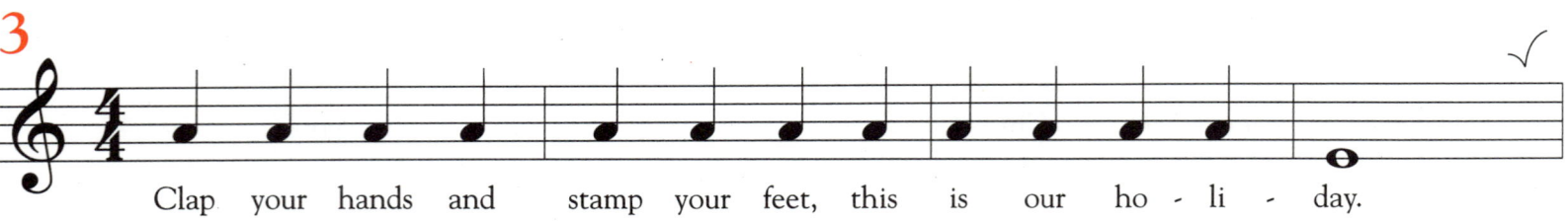
Clap your hands and stamp your feet, this is our ho - li - day.

Sing a song of hap - pi - ness and laugh your cares a - way.

It probably feels funny to have your
second right hand finger off its hole, for all of this page!

1

Remember: 𝄆 
means play it again

2

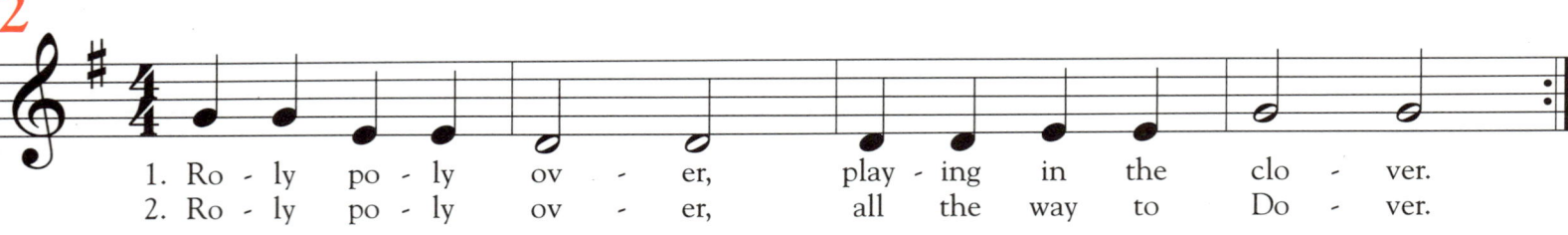

3

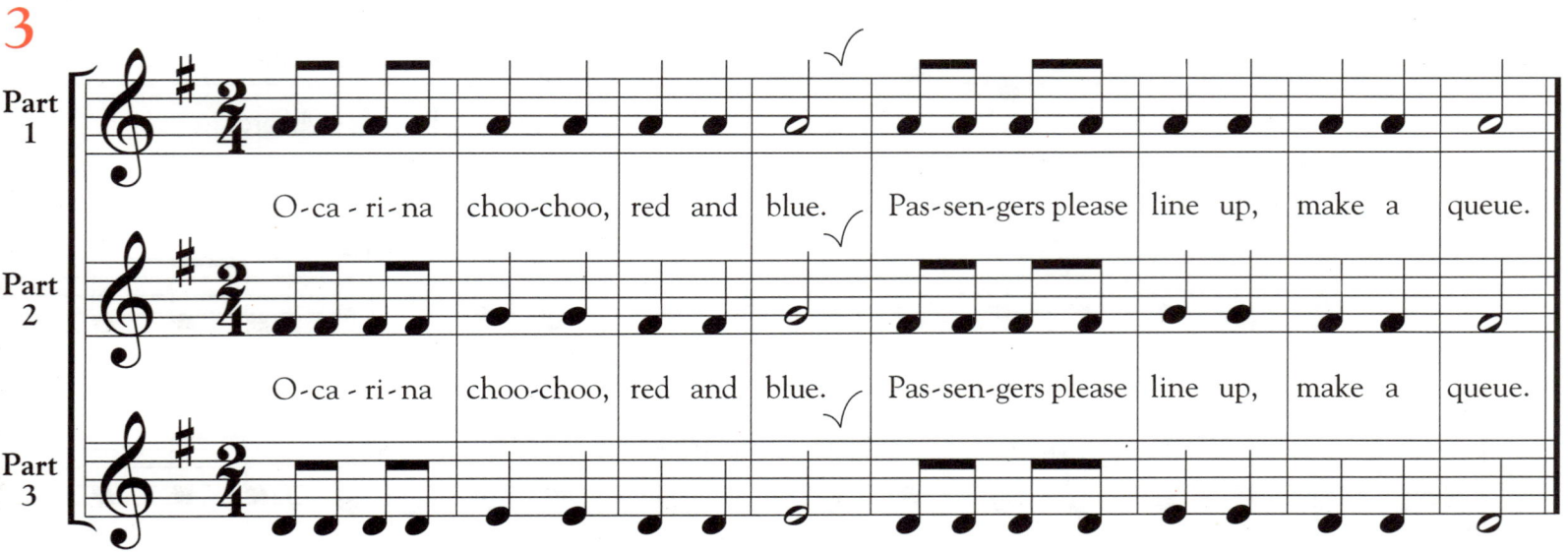

1

Birds fly high up in the sky, fish-es swim down in the sea.
Lamb-kins jump and skip and run on the hill-side, hav-ing fun.

2

Can you tell me what to do, when we get to Mar-well zoo?

D, E, F♯, G, A

Sometimes practise just the fingerings of a piece – with no blowing. Don't forget to use your balancers! (See p. 10)

Try a drum playing throughout this tune.
It could play the pattern twice before the ocarina begins

3
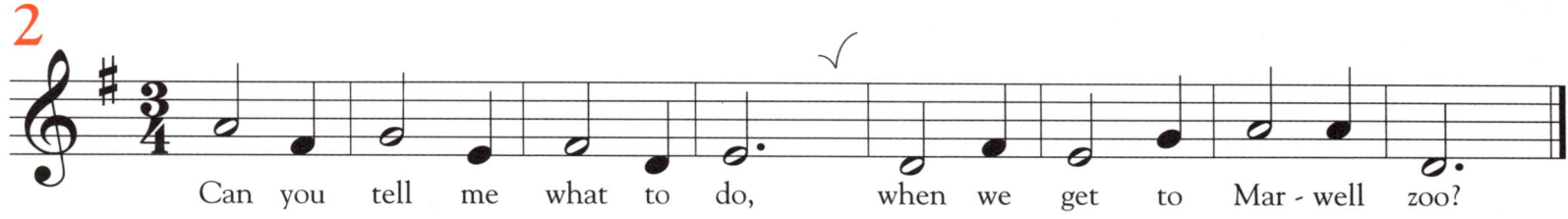
Hear the beat, made with feet, stamp-ing to their song.

In-dians dance round the fire, all night long.

D, E, F#, G, A

If you forget how to finger some of the notes, turn back, and take a look!

1

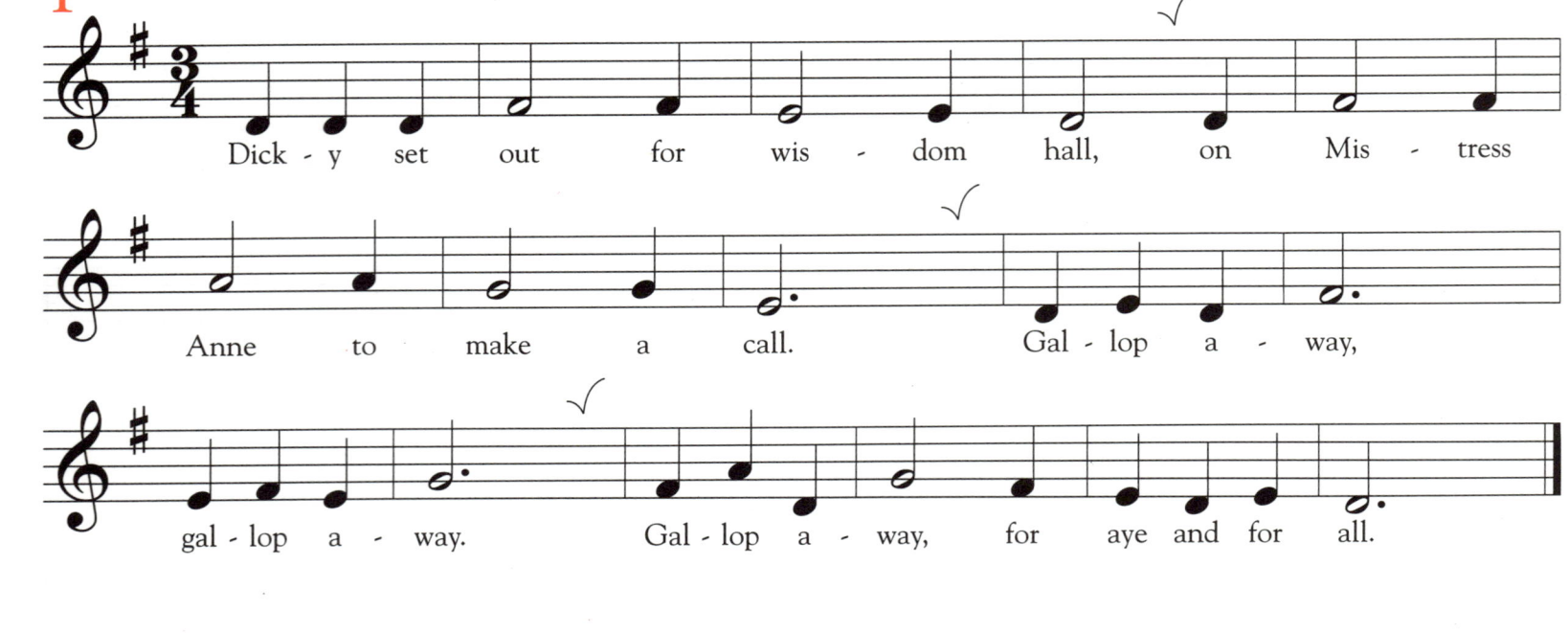

Dick-y set out for wis-dom hall, on Mis-tress Anne to make a call. Gal-lop a-way, gal-lop a-way. Gal-lop a-way, for aye and for all.

2

Lit-tle girl, lit-tle girl, where have you been? I've been gath-ering ro-ses to give to the Queen. Lit-tle girl, lit-tle girl, what gave she you? She gave me a dia-mond as big as a-ny shoe!

1

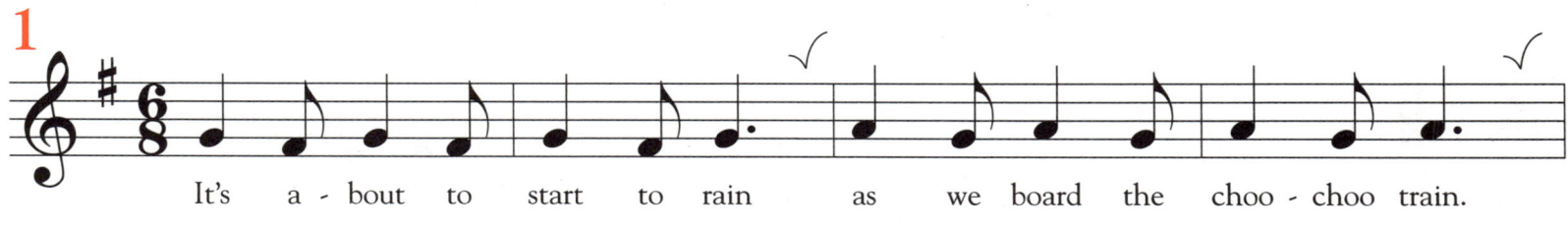

It's a - bout to start to rain as we board the choo - choo train.
It's a - bout to start to rain. We'll get wet!

2

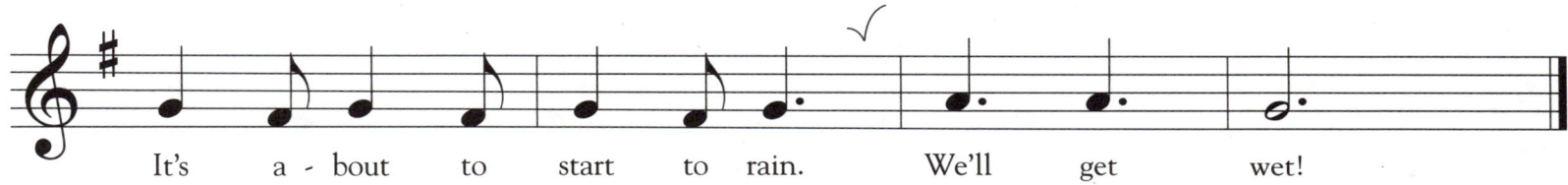

Stick - y tof - fee, ice - cream lol - ly. 1 2 3 4 shut that door!

3

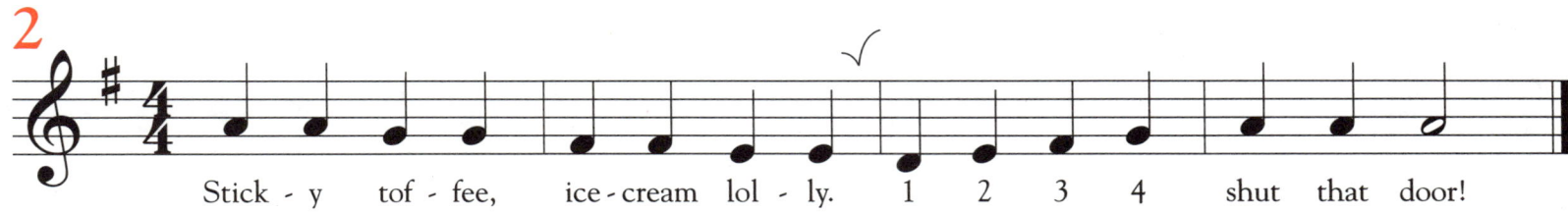

Here we go loo - by - loo. Here we go loo - by - light.
Here we go loo - by - loo, all on a Sat - ur - day night.

F♯, G, A

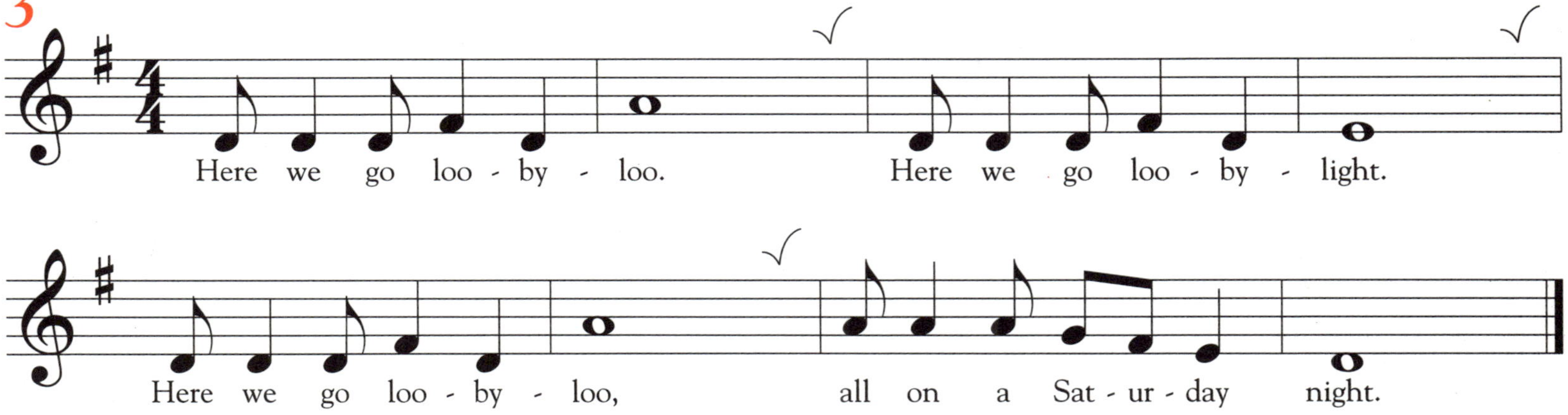

F♯ G A

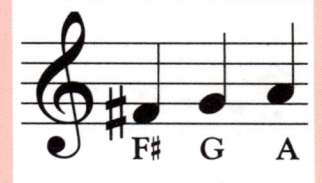

Are you still having fun playing wibbly-wobbly?

D, E, F♯, G, A

D E F♯ G A

F♯

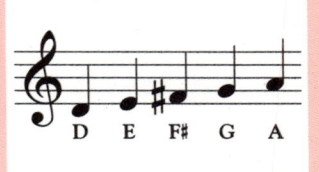

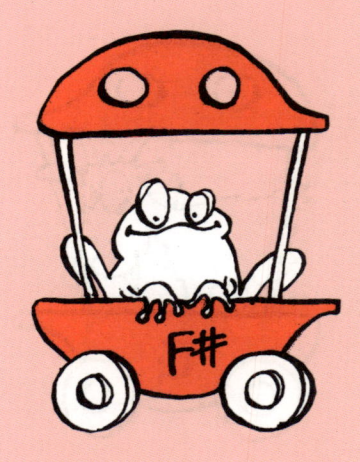

D, E, F♯, G, A

D
E
F♯
G
A

G

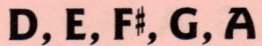

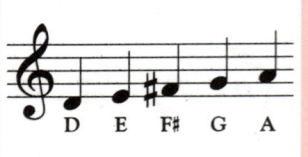

1

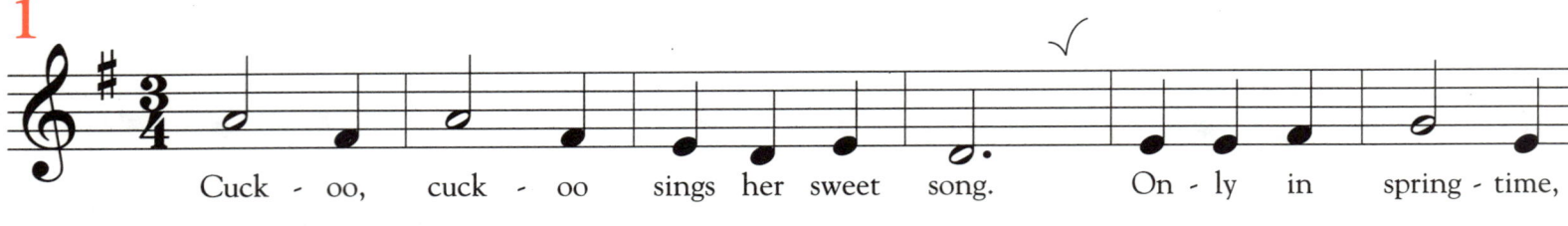

Cuck - oo, cuck - oo sings her sweet song. On - ly in spring - time,
on - ly in tree - tops. "Cuck - oo, cuck - oo" she nev - er stops!

2

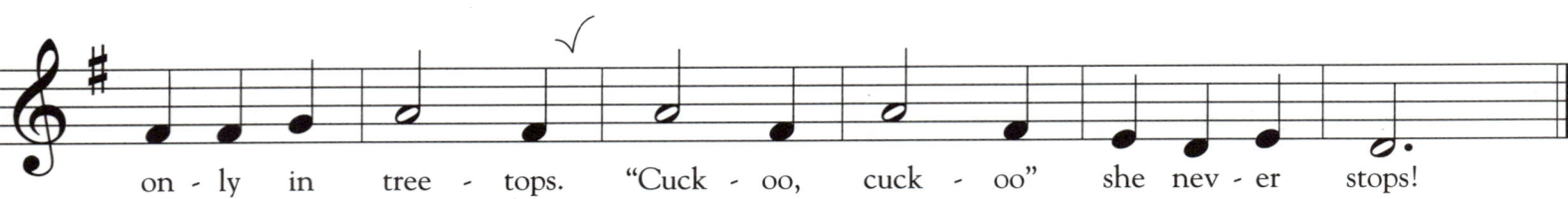

1. All a - board and tick - ets show! Hold on tight and off we go!
2. Don't lean out, keep well in - side, then we'll all en - joy the ride!

3

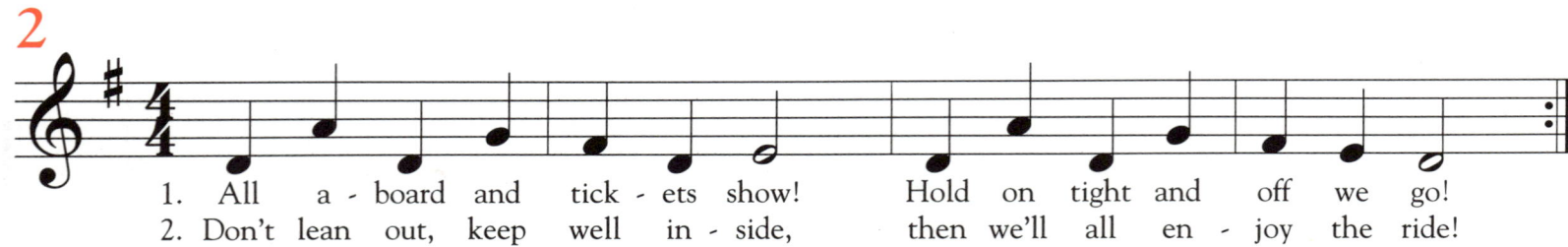

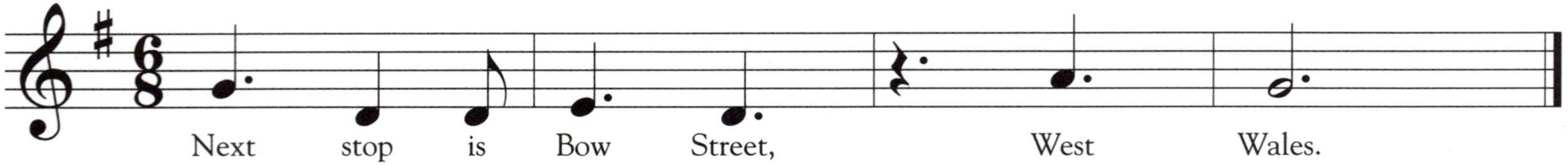

Next stop is Bow Street, West Wales.

𝄽· = a rest (no sound from the ocarina please!)

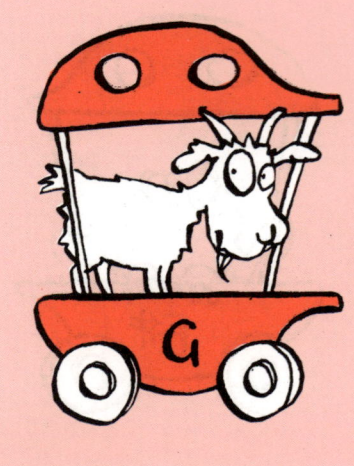

1

Girls and boys come out to play, the moon is shining as bright as day.
Leave your supper and leave your sleep, and join your playfellows in the street.

2

Two men went to mow, went to mow a meadow.
Two men, one man and his dog, went to mow a meadow.

3

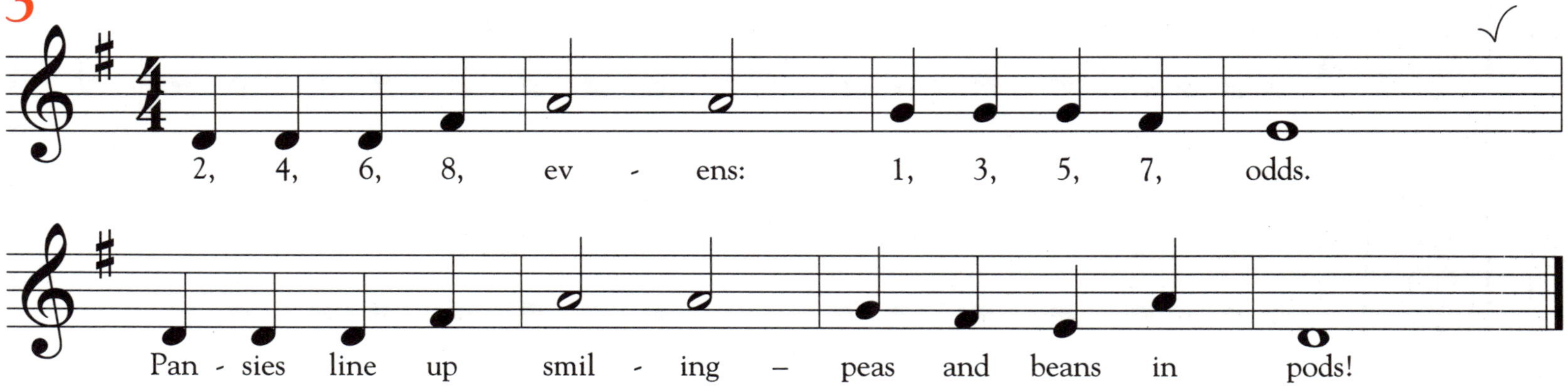

2, 4, 6, 8, evens: 1, 3, 5, 7, odds.
Pansies line up smiling – peas and beans in pods!

D, E, F#, G, A

A

F sharp G

D E

D

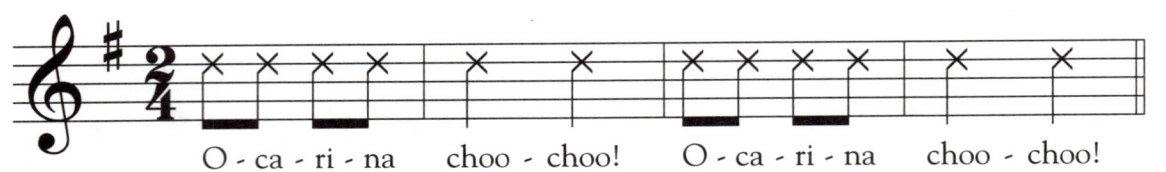

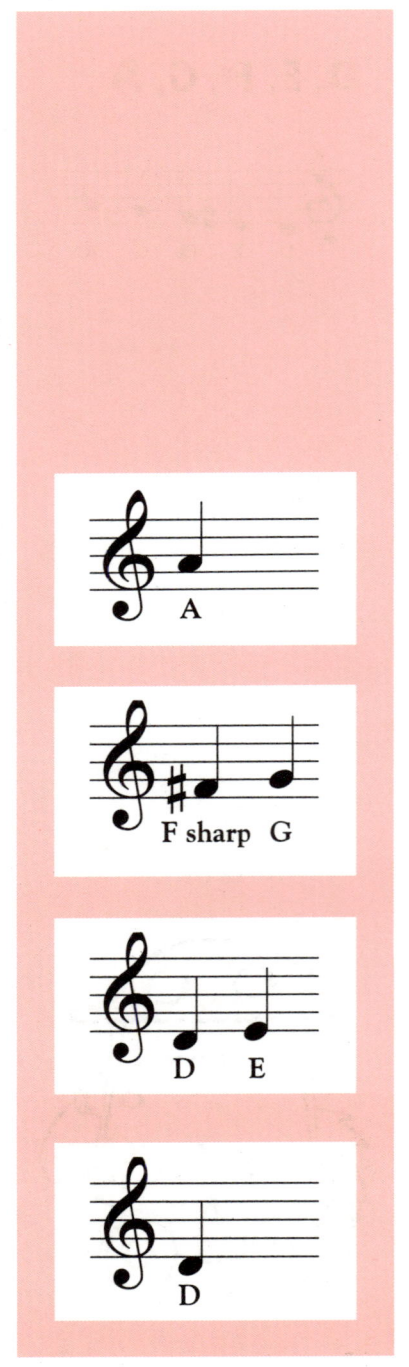

O - ca - ri - na choo - choo! O - ca - ri - na choo - choo!

The choo-choo whistle sound is made by uncovering all the finger holes. The whistle can also play along with the other parts.

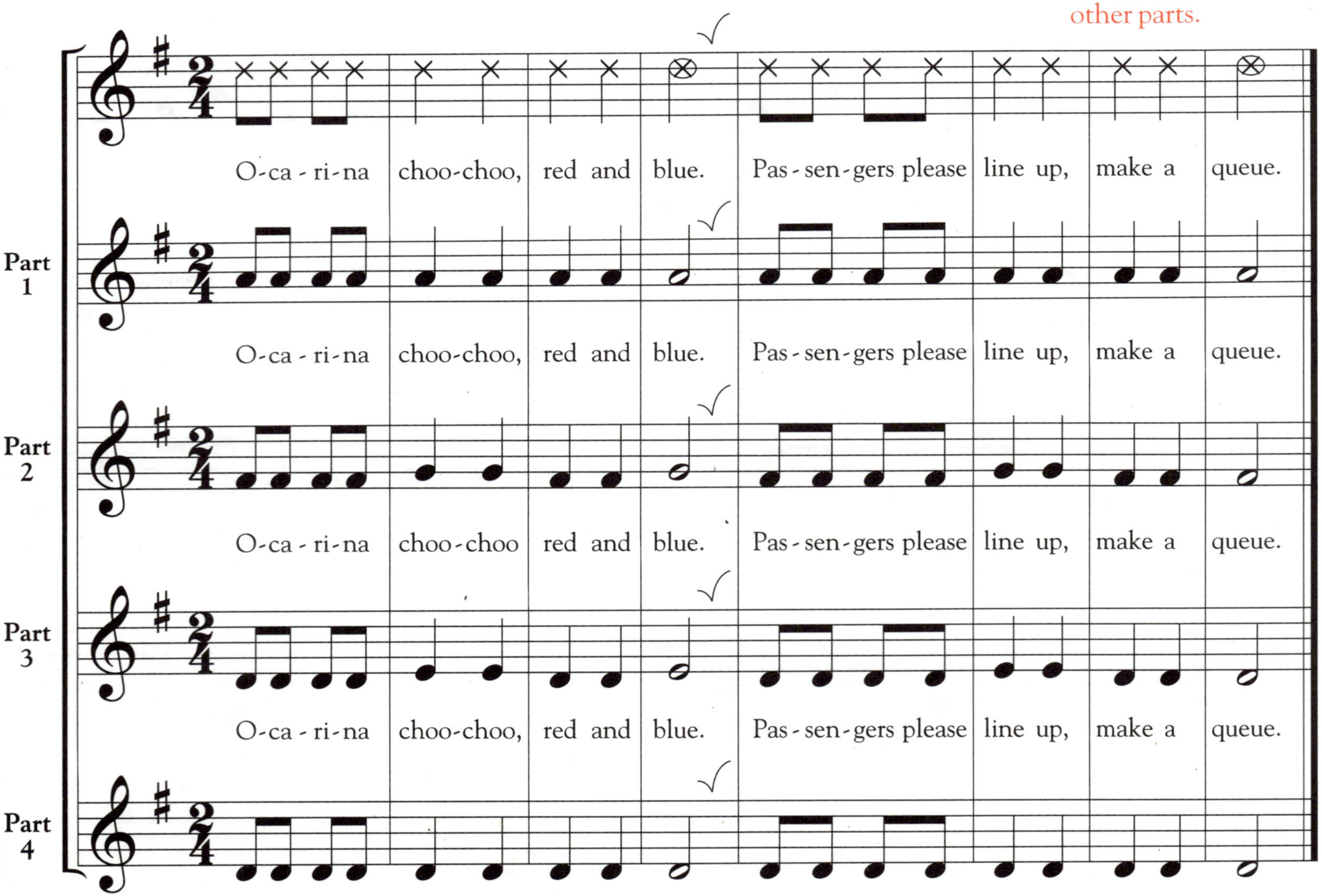
O-ca - ri-na choo-choo, red and blue. Pas - sen-gers please line up, make a queue.
Part 1
O-ca - ri-na choo-choo, red and blue. Pas - sen-gers please line up, make a queue.
Part 2
O-ca - ri-na choo-choo red and blue. Pas - sen-gers please line up, make a queue.
Part 3
O-ca - ri-na choo-choo, red and blue. Pas - sen-gers please line up, make a queue.
Part 4

Congratulations! You're now ready to move on to Ocarina Choo-Choo Book 2.

10/01 (41585)